MONEY MADNESS

by David A. Adler · illustrated by Edward Miller

Holiday House / New York

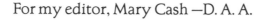

For my editor, Mary Cash —D. A. A.

To my friend, Ethan Royce —E. M.

The publisher wishes to thank Dan Davis of Staten Island
Coin Investors for his expert review of the coins used in
this book.

Text copyright © 2009 by David A. Adler
Illustrations copyright © 2009 by Edward Miller
All Rights Reserved
Printed and Bound in 10/09 at Tien Wah Press in Johor Bahru, Johor, Malaysia
The text typeface is Clemente Interro.
The artwork was created on the computer.
www.holidayhouse.com

10 9 8 7 6 5 4 3 2

Library of Congress Cataloging-in-Publication Data
Adler, David A.
Money madness / by David A. Adler ; illustrated by Edward Miller. — 1st ed.
p. cm.
ISBN 978-0-8234-1474-1 (hardcover) ISBN 978-0-8234-227-2 (paperback)
1. Money—History—Juvenile literature. 2. Money—Juvenile literature.
I. Miller, Edward, 1964-, ill. II. Title.
HG221.5.A346 2009
332.4—dc22
2008004223

Visit **www.davidaadler.com** for more information on the author, for
a listing of his books, and to download teacher's guides and educational
materials. You can also learn more about the writing process, take fun
quizzes, and read select pages from David A. Adler's books.

Visit **www.edmiller.com** for activities for kids and materials for teachers
and librarians that accompany this book. Join the Edward Miller Fan Club
to receive e-mail announcements of new books, projects, and contests.

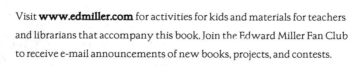

What's all this money madness?

People talk about money and work for it.

They seem to always want more of it.

Take a look at a dollar bill.

There's a nice portrait of

George Washington on it,

but it's just paper!

Why do people want money?

People want money because it can be used to buy things.

PRODUCE

MEATS

CHECKOUT

DELI

Now, imagine a world without money. If you were hungry and there was no such thing as money, how would you buy a loaf of bread? You would have to bake your own.

Without money, how would you get the ingredients for the bread? If no one would give or sell you flour, you would have to grow wheat, harvest it, grind it, and sift it before you would have flour for your bread.

If there was no such thing as money and you needed new clothes, you would have to make them.

Imagine if you had to knit your own sweater. Imagine if you had to raise a sheep and shear it, spin the wool to make the yarn, and then knit the sweater yourself.

There was a time before money. Long ago, people couldn't buy things. When they were hungry, they gathered berries and killed animals. When they were cold, they gathered wood for their fires.

Before there was money, people gathered and hunted for what they needed. They were self-sufficient.

Some people liked to hunt. They were good at it. Others were good at making clubs or clothing. Soon people traded one thing for another. A hunter traded with a food gatherer. A club maker traded with a clothing maker.

A system of trading one thing for another is called bartering.

Maybe you barter. Have you ever traded one toy for another? At lunch, have you ever traded an apple for an orange? That's bartering.

However, there are times when bartering doesn't work.
A hunter could trade an animal for berries, but how many berries?
And what if the hunter didn't want berries?

How would a baker trade for a house?

How many loaves of bread would he have to trade?

And why would anybody want so much bread?

Long before a person could eat all that bread, most of it would be stale.

A hunter who didn't want berries might be willing to trade for them anyway if he knew he could then trade the berries for something he did want.

A home owner might be willing to trade her house
for bread if she knew she could then trade the bread for
something she did want.

In those trades, the berries and bread would be
a kind of money.

At one time cows, sheep, camels, rocks, feathers, salt, dried fish, fishhooks, animal skins, and strings of beads made from clamshells were all used as money.

People valued cows, sheep, and camels. And they could always trade one of those animals for something they wanted.

But what if something was worth just half a cow? You wouldn't want to cut a cow in half to buy something.

What if the sheep or camel you wanted to trade was sickly? You might have trouble trading it.

When animals were used as money, your money needed to be fed. Your money could die. It could run away.

Rocks were another early form of money. Rocks come in different sizes, but they're heavy to carry around.

Feathers were used
as money too. Feathers
are light, but they can
blow away.

What was needed was
something that wouldn't
get sick, didn't have to be
fed, wasn't too heavy or
light, came in different
weights or sizes, and most
people wanted.

Hundreds of years ago, people found that metals made good money. People valued bronze and copper, which could be cut into small pieces just right for carrying around.

To know how much each piece was worth, people just had to weigh it. The heavier the piece of metal, the more it was worth.

These pieces became the first coins.

Then coins were made
from silver and gold.
People wanted silver
and gold, so they were
happy to trade for
silver and gold coins.

But carrying many coins is difficult,
so paper money was invented.

The first paper money was like a printed promise, a promise that the money could be taken to a bank and traded for silver and gold coins.

In the United States people no longer use silver and gold coins as money.

But paper money still has value, because you can use it to buy things.

You can use paper money to buy bread, furniture, and clothing. You can use it to buy a house. You can even use paper money to buy silver and gold.

OPEN

BANK
HOLIDAY
JULY 4

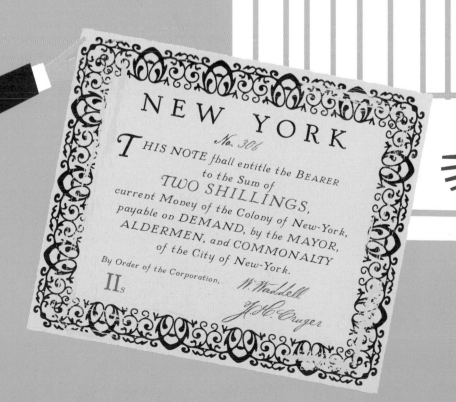
NEW YORK
No. 306
THIS NOTE fhall entitle the BEARER
to the Sum of
TWO SHILLINGS,
current Money of the Colony of New-York,
payable on DEMAND, by the MAYOR,
ALDERMEN, and COMMONALTY
of the City of New-York.
By Order of the Corporation,
II_s
W. Waddell
H.C. Cruger

Each country has its own money.

In the United States people use dollars.

In Mexico people use pesos, in Israel new shekels,
in Russia rubles, in China yuan, in Canada dollars, in
South Africa rand, and in Brazil reais.

People in many of the countries in Europe use euros.

1. Peso, 2. New Shekel, 3. Ruble, 4. Yuan, 5. Canadian Dollar, 6. Rand, 7. Real, 8. Euro

The value of money in each country keeps changing. One U.S. dollar may be worth ten Mexican pesos one day and a little more or less the next day.

Your dollar may be worth seven Chinese yuan one day and slightly more or less the next day.

2 dollars

1 dollar

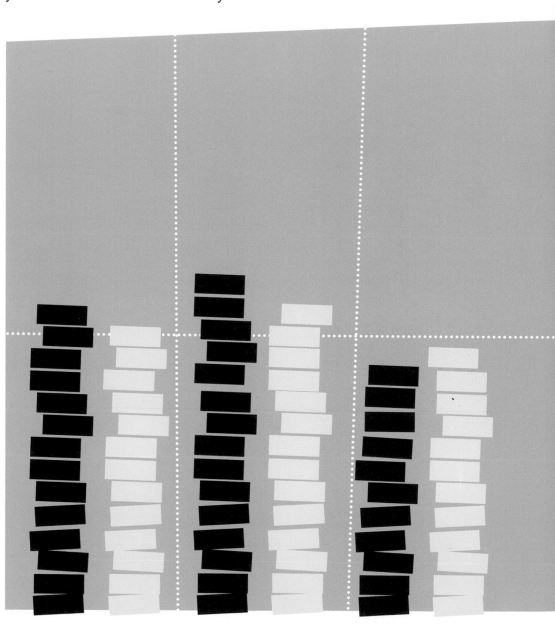

■ Mexican peso

☐ Chinese yuan

Monday　　**Tuesday**　　**Wednesday**

The value of each country's money goes up when prices go down in that country. When that happens, the dollar buys more.

The value of each country's money goes down when prices go up in that country. When prices go up, the same dollar buys less.

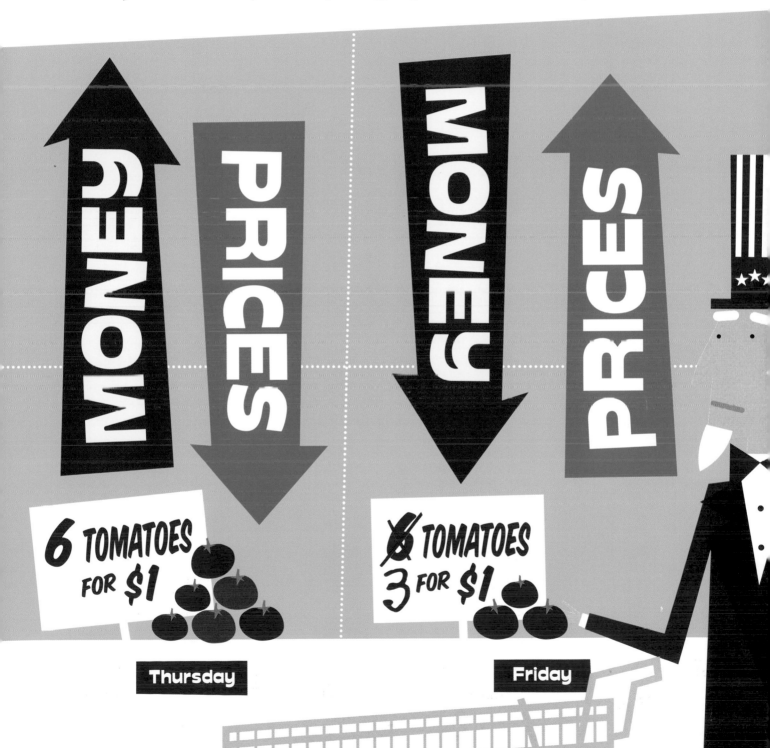

When prices go down, the value of a dollar goes up. For example, when a scoop of ice cream costs one dollar, each dollar buys one scoop. If prices go down and a scoop of ice cream now costs just fifty cents, a dollar buys double what it bought before. Now a dollar buys two scoops of ice cream. The value of a dollar in relation to ice cream went up.

As prices in a country go down, not just for ice cream but for many, even most, things, the value of its currency goes up.

Checks and credit cards are money too, because they can be used to buy things.

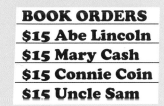

BOOK ORDERS
$15 Abe Lincoln
$15 Mary Cash
$15 Connie Coin
$15 Uncle Sam

BANK ACCOUNT
Name: Uncle Sam
Funds: $100
Purchase: − $ 15
$ 85

Some people even use digital money. With digital money there is a computer record of the money in an account. When you spend that money to buy a book or download music, the amount you spend is subtracted from your account.

COIN Collecting for Beginners $15 BUY

Even though you cannot see digital money, it's still money because it can be used to buy things.

We no longer live in a world with just hunters and food gatherers.
We live in a world with dancers, teachers, doctors, astronauts, dentists,
and bakers.

Without money, it's hard to imagine what a dancer would trade
to buy a car.

Without money, it's hard to imagine what a teacher would trade to buy a sweater. It's hard to imagine a world without money.

I ♥ US

Now reach into your pockets. Do you have any coins? Do you have any paper money? If you do, you're probably pleased.

You know with money you can buy things you want. With money you can buy things you need.